JN411153

Syncopation

Syncopation

A collection of new poems by Kim Sono
Translated by Eunice Lee

싱코페이션 김선오

K-Poet Series 040

ASIA

Contents

SYNCOPATION

K POET

Like cloud like wall

The room was white but the window was wide
so the white might've been outside
It might've been a white cloth or a white wall
but we were inside the room and soon
we could see the whitish tops of our feet
In them, blood vessels, and in the vessels, blood
would've been flowing but our feet never
opened
The cloud said "okay" and flowed into the room
The tops of our feet were almost wiped out of
sight
When I saw your face
your face was congealed
neither red nor blue

either cloth or wall or both
mimicking me or maybe not
You made that face
and I laughed; like music
my mouth was drawn as a crescent
Your arm was a crescent, my arm was a crescent
The room was white but it was just right for a
    hug

Like cloud like wall
Like cloud like wall

The room was bright but the light might've
    been outside

Things hard to tell apart in the dark

I went to a bright place. The dog cat turtle followed
behind me. I turned around to Min Jeong Jun
A B C were my grass sansevieria mimosa
and I watered the garden
slowly accepting the fact that each droplet
sprinkled from the hose was a ball of light.

Of the dog cat turtle
I'd never lived with a dog cat
I didn't vibe with grass sansevieria
I'd once fallen asleep under a mimosa
and when I went to the bright place,
there was light

falling between mimosa leaves.
Eyelids became light puddles.
Min Jeong Jun
the names were calling me
joking that they'd all
come over into my dream.
I liked that joke.

A you bring your palms together
B you twist your palms against each other
C you open and turn up both palms

Translator's Note: ABC is a Korean game in which players take turns shouting a letter of the alphabet (typically "A," "B," or "C") to which other player(s) must quickly respond with the corresponding hand sign. All players begin by bringing their palms together (the "A" sign), and one of them chants "A, A," followed by a letter of their choice. For instance, if one player yells "A, A...C!" other(s) must respond with the "C" sign, which is to turn up both palms. Whoever makes the wrong hand sign loses.

No

On this road I can't show you that road.

No words to describe it.

Just follow me this way.

It was burdensome trying to become myself

Like this. I tried unfolding the bird. It was
already unfolded when I unfolded it
and when I unfolded the dog-ear it left behind
a line. Like this. Indicating the right-hand page.
A transparent line and two corners formed a
triangle in which
the number 9 was locked. Like this.
The dog-ear kept folding itself back into a dog-
ear.
It flapped. It needed no wind. Breathe
slowly to live longer.
Like this. Follow me. Unfold your lungs. Unfold
them and that much
of the world will enter you. Animals that

breathe slowly live longer. Like this
bird unfolded
breath
-ing
huff
puff
huff
puff

Unfold
what's already unfolded
Try unfolding it

Bird and I

Bird and I exercise
Bird and I
Bird and I
Bird and I

(When I turned the last page, it felt like the end of the world but that was because I'd been holding my breath the whole time I was reading I thought I'd forgotten how to breathe but I remembered soon enough though I didn't know if it was the same way I'd breathed before)

A certain nuance

I ate at a restaurant I didn't know Walked down streets I didn't know A brick I didn't know A person I didn't know A ball I didn't know Flew towards me I kicked it in a position I didn't know In a direction I didn't know On an evening I didn't know And I left my dead friend's Kakao chatroom by accident

Clouds leaving clouds and time leaving clocks and what were your favorite gifs again They were so cute I really wanted to save them

You and I were walking in a schoolyard I didn't know A sunset I didn't know sat on your face

As we swept away swarms of bugs I didn't know You don't have to know Said your shadow As it warped into a shape I might've known In a memory I didn't know

A wound I didn't know healed without my knowing Why are you crying looool You laughed and I laughed along looool There has to be a video with your voice in it, but no matter how I scroll and scroll through my photos it won't show up

The red behind my eyelids

This photo, I think
I was four? Five?
I remember Mom saying
Grandma will be here
She'll be here She'll be here
she said and I waited
She'll be here She'll be here
Mom's voice in the kitchen
ring ring ringing then
suddenly Mom was gone
Grandma wasn't
here yet The front door
was shut and light came
through the little kitchen window

A square of light quivered
on the floor and I played with it
stuck my hand in it
lay my face on it Oh so warm
She'll be here She'll be here
And then Grandma really
was here
I thought she'd never be here
or Mom would be here first
or I would be here alone
forever or something
That's why I was playing with the light
But then Grandma was here
The front door opened

and Grandma, well,
her nose was bleeding
Her nose
bled bled bled
red on the floor
drip drop
Grandma ran
towards me
grabbed a towel or was it a dishrag
and pinched her nose
but the blood drip dropped
down the rag
into the sink onto her white clothes
into the square of light the blood

drip dropped
Grandma smiled
wiping off the blood
I remember this photo
I think I was four?
Five? I might be wrong
Maybe I made all of this up
Maybe this is Grandma at my house
posing for a photo with me in her arms
Maybe this is a story I made up just because
the weather looks nice through the window in
the photo
But that was my first time
seeing blood you see?

A child seeing blood
That doesn't happen very often does it?
The blood was such a bright red and so
I remember it
but I might be wrong
I'm wearing a cap in the photo
so I might've been back from a walk
Someone must have taken the photo Mom
probably or Dad
Probably wasn't just me and Grandma there
But my memory tells me
This is a photo from the day
I saw blood for the first time
This was the first blood of my life

That's how I see it

Blood dripping into light

I've never seen anything like that since

♦

♦

Such a tint of pink in the sky can be seen only briefly, or not at all on many days. That sunset-to-be, might we call that a blood-tinted sky? If so, then at that hour, in a park by the Han River, there must have been a radio, clueless about how it had ended up there, and that old-fashioned (rectangular, metallic, hefty, many-buttoned) radio must have been broadcasting a voice. It would have rung far and wide. Someone would have heard it, recorded it. Missed parts of it. And yet.

Silence

And yet the lot was empty.

Mother, Mom, Tylenol, mild excitement, evening slowly turning into morning, Kim Yun-yeong tripping on my foot and falling, This stop is Sajikdan, Children's Library, fifteen side profiles and mouths open to a burger, a white-haired, white-haired chihuahua, Matsuda Yukimasa's *Adventure of the Eye*, Eternity Apartments, one thousand snowflakes piling on the alleyway footsteps, teabag threads tangled in a box of Osulloc Moon Walk Tea, the carrying, carried, grass lawn of the National Museum of Modern and Contemporary Art and the rat,

my hand holding a beautifully napping rat,
hole, green steel locker, Pepero in rectangular
darkness, you at the point where you're almost
gone, walking around Gwanghwamun Square
with our fingers interlocked, party, fountain,
migraine, Seong-jin Cho's Handel album,

ready to burst in sunset colors, a place flooded
with grief and senseless longing, scattered with
many steel bars and wood blocks . . .

Matter and memory

Many

many rooms, so I knew that this wasn't a tunnel.

A door opened towards

Sunday. Sunday trapped me in Jongno.

Spring was coming to Sajik Park. There was

that tree we called our tree. The tree

too young to be called a flowering tree

was rattling spring. We stepped with our left,

no, right feet,

no, your left and right depend on where you're
facing, so

let's just say we were walking. Sajik Park

is followed by Sajik Tunnel.

We were attached to our tree. We were also

tugged into the tunnel.

Sajik Tunnel opens towards

the afternoon, and there

a tree we don't call our tree will drop

a leaf,

two leaves

three roads

on the tops of our feet.

Oh so cold,

Our mouths will open

as we swim

in a deep clear pool.

The water will reflect a cloud

and we will call it our tree.

Torn water closes up quickly. The way I

cleave my bare back to yours.

Many times

we splashed our feet in the water, and I knew
that this wasn't a dream.

That I don't like dreams that are wet.

The tree is skinny.

I wonder if the tree might be us.

Or just a tree.

The bottle of the bright hill

The tree faces the chair
as if looking down at its future

The light moves through the plastic bottle
across the grassy field

The bottle looks down at the light

The young water
feels its own flesh when held

The flesh feels like the future
Is shaped like the light
spilled on the ground

The chair faces the tree
as if looking up at its memory

The bottle rolls downhill
The light rolls after the bottle

When the sky looks down at the bottle
the sky's clavicle unlocks

The sound startles the water
The water spills out of the bottle

The sky laughs

Hands to the young water
the darkening bone

Same bone different sea

This boat is a white boat
that passes by my house, from island to shore
from shore to island, rippling the water
Bananas and soccer balls and
Grandpa's ashes in a box and seagulls
were things it carried
This boat is a red boat
that passes by my house, from here
to the island, from the island to the horizon
rippling the water on its way
The boat is red because
I stand on the seashore usually at
sunset, and this boat
is a black boat that passes by my house

and this is an island
Grandpa drove the boat
loaded with bananas
and soccer balls for me, from this island
to that island and back
This boat is a blue boat
that passes by my house
from the island all the way here
from here all the way to the island
flicking off sunlight,
splitting its way through
blue and white ripples . . .
I stood on the seawall at sunset
and cried Grandpa!

at the returning boat
Lights blinked
This boat is a boat that passes by my house
Today it carries my ashes in a box
ashore
from a place no longer home
to the horizon
to islands to shores
to bananas and soccer balls
and the place where everything is

"I told you to scatter mine in the sea"
"Sorry I can't   It's illegal"

Ha ha ha ha
White frothing
splashes of water
The smiling faces I see inside them

One two three four
Everything can be seen from the sky
and one seagull cries

The boundary as an aesthetic choice

Bird was a good person. When I came out, it showed me its dead body. I understood. The problem of being a boy or girl or neither didn't seem as serious as the problem of being both dead and alive.

It was less like having both a dead body and a living body than losing both, as I understood it. Just like I was losing out on both the female and the male. Bird was troubled by the fact that both its life and its death were leaking between its wings. I could claim my existence by using the word "nonbinary" (despite its being a mere negation of the word "binary"), or by asking to be referred to by "they" pronouns, but what do you even call that state of being alive and dead at once?

Bird was neither ghost nor zombie, just a bird carrying around its own dead body. Where did Bird keep it? Neglected, the body would rot and give off a terrible odor, others would easily find out, and the cops would arrest Bird. Nor could Bird throw the body out. But what is a bird supposed to tell a cop? "Killing a bird is not considered a crime in this country. Is this a violation of the Animal Protection Act? But what about all the people who eat chicken? Also, this dead body happens to be me."

If it weren't a city bird, Bird could have claimed an uninhabited island for itself and laid out some five hundred of its own dead bodies. Dead bird bodies drying out under the sun . . . Bird would have flown across the beach to make sure all the bodies were drying well . . . Occasionally plugging an eyeball back into its socket . . .

Just like I'd gone to a women's studies professor, Bird had gone to a linguist.

"Your name in English is *Bird*, and the Korean

word for it is pronounced *sae*, or *say*, so you could choose between the two spellings, but do keep in mind that in French this is *sé*."

There was Tamil, there was Hebrew, there was Bengali, and so on, but Bird was fine with learning just two foreign languages. Learning more languages meant understanding more words on trips abroad, but this also meant Bird would no longer be able to shut words out of its ears, even in a different part of the world. Bird was satisfied translating most foreign words at the *blah blah blah* level.

Bird felt nonbinary between life and death. Every boundary is a kind of silence, said Bird, wearing a good-fellow smile.

I didn't ask, Where did you get that dead body?

It was less like losing both than letting go of both, as I understood it. This was my aesthetic choice. Bird gave me a pat on the shoulder. I gave Bird a pat on the wing. We each went back home.

A weak unsettled life

Come back. I lay on the sunbed. Come back, come back. I tossed and turned. The swimming pool lay unfolded. I could see it while lying down and while sitting up. I didn't know when I'd fallen asleep. Or when I'd woken up. But the swimming pool felt real. It was softly stirring its clouds. Come back. What? I turned my head towards the voice. There was an angel. An angel sitting in lotus pose with one eye closed. It wasn't my partner. Nor was it anyone in my friend group. Come back, said the voice that technically should have been the angel's, ringing through the forest. The forest? I'd booked a resort for a hundred and twenty dollars a night.

When I remembered this, the forest turned into a cheap resort. I heard construction noises. You want me to cut down his five-hundred-year-old tree? Someone's baffled cry. Come back, the drill said to me. Or rather, the words "Come back" sounded like a drill. The angel with one eye closed did not have a mouth. The angel with one eye closed charged forward, diving into the water. The skinny angel soared midair, wearing a bright blue bikini. Come back, come back . . . Ripping the cloud's reflection on the water, the angel vanished. The resort stood where a five-hundred-year-old tree was cut down and if I'd known this, I wouldn't have booked it.

Would've gone for a walk in the woods instead. Would've walked and walked and walked. The angel with one eye closed peeked out of the water. I looked at its open eye and beckoned with my finger. Come back, babe.

The angel with one eye closed walked out of the water. Water dripped from its wings as it returned to our holiday. The forest must have had a horizon. The sun must have hung on it. That red hue lengthening left and right could have been sunrise or sunset. The closed eye of the angel must have held a pupil, which someone must have called the sun. The angel lay with me as I watched the side of its face turn red, watched another sun set and rise in the droplets of water on its skin. The angel still had one eye closed. What is life without this? Our laughter stirred the trees. Or rather, the stir of the trees was our laughter. I watched a leaf fall slowly from the tree to the angel's face, looked at the leaf-turned-lip, then threw up.

A soft greeting

Trees glitter. Are there such things as glittering trees? Unni's* gate is made of glittering wood. There are more friends than I'd thought. I'm surprised.

Unni brings a glass of water. I drink the water. The cup glitters. The wet lips glitter. There is a bed. A picture frame. I'm surprised again. Unni tells me and the friends a joke. Three friends or four. Unni doesn't laugh much. Unni is very tall, and when I look up at her she looks down at me.

Three or four friends. Me, Unni. A framed picture of a cat. A cat that is no more. Two or three cats climb across our laps. I become Unni and then me. Then a friend who might be Unni.

Outside the window, a huge tree. A shadow, the cloud's or the gate's, falls on my face, and Unni makes fun of me. It's like I have a beard. I think maybe I should just turn into a cat but that doesn't seem to work. The cat's name is Olleh. My name is Seona.

What's yours, Unni? And Unni looks at me with a face maybe angry or maybe smiling. White hairs on school uniforms. In the laps of the three or four friends. Same cat. Same friends. Me, Unni. Under the dark wooden ceiling we all burst into laughter at once, and this I remember as glitter.

A poem I wrote before going to Unni's funeral.

Translator's Note: The term "unni" refers to a big sister, female relative, or admired older girl.

Coming before going

On Earth this is called a blizzard, and amid these gusts of snow a single most fragile most delicate snowflake falls on Earth slowly, ever so slowly, in a trajectory uninterrupted by other snowflakes, but you swivel in whirlwinds quite a bit before you escape into a fog, and the moment you look skyward the fog might look like a single large snowflake. It might look like a hangnail dangling on a cloudy sky but in truth it's falling, slowly running down a boundary and when its movement meets your gaze, the snowflake vibrates a bit. Into your pupil settles a shadow, deeper than the vibration but very small and white, soon to vanish. This fog is the faith you hold before knowing you're looking at the sky, the love that protects you from the shock that is the sky, the dizziness that dampens such refusals and emotions, the joy of being spared from the sky thanks to the fog's hospitality. And so you can look up, from among the dead trees in the empty lot, and greet the gusts of snow falling on you. And you are falling on the gusts of snow, too. Words must be piling and piling in your mind. For instance, the word "blizzard." Faces must be piling and piling in a pale sequence. Piercing these faintly colored faces a single sudden most fragile most delicate snowflake falls on your eyelid and makes a subtle melting sound, and hearing this sound you predict that this memory will be unforgettable, but your prediction is blown to bits and reduced to the sorts of colors that aid emotions in memories of spaces, like the ashy color of dead tree skin, yet it's these colors that soften the word "blizzard," soften its edges a bit, and you look down again. You leave the empty lot. A certain memory, chilled and dampened a bit, continues as you walk.

A bit of the forest

There is a rocky mountain. A peak. A small cave. In which you sit. Your eyes are closed. You face the cave's mouth. You see light and dark clash with your body in between. Your eyes are closed. You feel the subtle vibration of your eyelashes. Your eyes are closed. You see the forest unfolding under your feet and the sky unfolding overhead and the cave in which you sit and you see all of these at once. Your eyes are closed. You feel at once the cold inside the cave and the heat outside the cave. Your eyes are closed. You see at once the days and the nights on the rocky mountain. Your eyes are closed. You see at once the blood-red sun and the crashing rain. Your eyes are closed. You see the moments of contact preceding your formation. Your eyes are closed. You see the movements of consonants and vowels gathering into your name. Your eyes are closed. You hear at once all the countless voices calling for you. Your eyes are closed. You watch the voices scattering in the skies and on the earth becoming rain sounds and wind sounds. Your eyes are closed. You see the rain's will and the wind's will. Your eyes are closed. Your gaze crashes into a corner of the forest against your will. Your eyes are closed. You feel protected. Your eyes are closed. Grandma sleeps. Your eyes are closed. You see yourself five or so years old trying to sleep next to her and the quivering square of sunlight on the blanket. Your eyes are closed. Your gaze shoots skyward. Your eyes are closed. The gaze crashes again into a corner of the forest. Your eyes are closed. You see your floating reflection on a train window, yourself in a school uniform. Your eyes are closed. Translucent views move through your reflection. Your eyes are closed. You gaze after yourself walking on a white sand beach. Your eyes are closed. You see an empty lot where all the books you've ever read lie unfolded. Your eyes are closed. You see that every page in every book is an empty lot. Your eyes are closed. You hear shrieks among the waves. Your eyes are closed. It occurs to you that you might've witnessed a death, but you can't see what you don't wish to see. Your eyes are closed. Your gaze shoots skyward. Your eyes are closed. You see parts of the forest burning, then the burnt parts growing back their greenery. Your eyes are closed. Your gaze crashes. Your eyes are closed. You see your white-haired self sitting on a lakeside bench reading a book. Your eyes are closed. The wind turns the pages, one by one. Your eyes are closed. You see several snowflakes melting on the surface of the lake then quickly becoming part of the lake. Your eyes are closed. You see your family members coming to life then dying. Your eyes are closed. You see your friends coming to life then dying. Your eyes are closed. You see a tear flowing out of your eye. Your eyes are closed. You see that your past and future are part of this forest. Your eyes are closed. You see that things neither of your past nor of your future are part of this forest. Your eyes are closed. You see your eternally closed eyelids. Your eyes are closed.

You open your eyes. The house is quiet.

No subtitles

How a wall sprang up in the middle of the
  living room
I have no clue

Just moments ago we were eating fried rice
watching Netflix
had a bit of food left

With a puzzled face you look around the wall
the black-and-white photos on all its four
  corners

Young Winona Ryder Leslie Cheung Monica
  Bellucci Al Pacino

We touch their faces

barely remembering the titles of their films
Most of these folks must have had lead roles
I haven't seen *Days of Being Wild* or *Godfather*
Suddenly the house folds

The house becomes a photo album
The grains of fried rice flatten
We skip from this page to that
see that our living room wedding photo
is now a photo within a photo

Why is this washing machine standing on an

endless desert
Why is our puppy printed on Monica Bellucci's
t-shirt
Why is Leslie Cheung lying seductively on this
IKEA sofa

I know you once dreamed of becoming an actor
but this is too absurd to be the aftermath of
your dream

Makes no sense right
You smile a gummy smile

How old are these people

Are they dead or alive

You take out your phone to look them up

Leslie Cheung gets up from the sofa
grabs your phone and says
No, don't look us up, and smiles

He's in a tank top
We decide to have a drink with him
Winona's been on a sober streak since last
month
Al Pacino sleeps like a baby

We have a lot of homemade wines
It's an old hobby of mine
Gyul is a Korean tangerine

The gyul wine gets Leslie dancing
Belated congrats on your wedding
He kisses the back of my hand and yours

Pages turn rapidly
Too many stories to tell

By the time we're on the last page of this house
we're all drunk

Gyul wine all over the floor and nowhere to put
 our feet

I can't remember
How old are we again
Let's look it up

Can you pass my phone

In front of a switched-off TV
you and a white-haired Leslie fast asleep

Syncopation

"If we could look down at the face of a sleeping god, if we could see the god's body shuddering against nightmares, the god's tears coursing down the god's quaking chest and cheekbones, we would eventually learn that the world collapsing all at once in the god's dream is this place on which we stand, and we would be terrified."

Ah Ah Ah

Dark clouds were easy to make
when the earth was staring at me

Bellyached rabbits were easy to make

by knotting grass into balls

Papa, Papa wasn't
that hard to make either

Ah Ah Ah

Papa gave me a rock to skip
one two three four
and that was easy too

I ate slept made rain while

Papa vanished and rivers vanished

and hiccupping rabbits vanished

Bells rang in temple ruins
and it was easy to meditate

Ah Ah Ah

The hardest thing to do
was to come up with names

I could've cried out the names
tugging them loose like threads

Dreams would've peeled off dreams

like a sweater losing its dimensions

Instead
I made a dog
made it bark at my stomach

Ah Ah Ah

It tickled me so hard I laughed
It tickled me so hard, the world

Ah Ah Ah

Ah Ah Ah

Like beauty without content

1)

2)

3)

4)

5)

6)

7)

Like glittering sleet
on the back of a lamb (羊)

1) I stopped lotioning myself to watch a white plastic bag flying outside my window. I watched the bag soar up among buildings and fly in the blue. The bag shook as if to fall then flew back up again and again. I lowered my face to finish lotioning it. When I turned my gaze back to my window the bag was gone and in its place flew a bird.

2) I can't remember how the dream started. My memory starts with me in the middle of the dream. Where has the prelude to my dream disappeared? Where something has been erased, eraser marks remain. Objects I think I've lost forever sometimes reappear. Maybe the dream's missing prelude becomes reality the moment I leave my dream, unfolding itself before my eyes. The reality in which I live is the beginning of a dream I can't remember. If you look closely at eraser marks you can see the erased letters. Sometimes you can't.

3) Grandma's nose is bleeding. I can't understand why this sort of scene is my first memory. But Grandma's nose was, no doubt, bleeding, and she tried to pinch her nose with a towel but the red blood drip dropped. I was four years old or five. Memory began. As if beaten up by the image of blood.

4) I don't know how long I've been here. Or where I am.

5) If you raise the pitch of a sound beyond the audible frequency range for humans, the sound eventually turns into light. We might think of light as sounds we've once heard. If you convert the visual data of a beautiful landscape into sound it becomes a terrible noise. If you convert the audio data of beautiful music into an image it becomes an awful scribble. What leap has taken place between the beautiful and the terrible? Is life the destination of the universe that leaps out of nothingness? Is this well-wrought nothingness my face?

6) On a field of snow are countless desks. I sit at one of them. I am given a book, a piece of paper, and a pen. This must mean I should copy the book by hand. I open it. I read. I copy. But the pen has no ink. Nothing is written on the paper. And yet I read. I copy. Nothing is written on the paper. Traces are engraved by the tip of the pen. Sometimes they're not.

7) The character "羊" means both "auspicious" and "wandering."

Walkology

Here's an experiment I want to try. You lock a newborn baby in a room and play Bach. The child is locked in a windowless room listening to nothing but Bach until it's all grown up. It can't listen to any words, or other sounds, or other kinds of music. It listens to everything by Bach, every variation of every piece, from the Glenn Gould album to that botched performance on YouTube by the young white guy wearing glasses (the high F sharp doesn't even work on his broken Yamaha keyboard) and the child must listen to everything without skipping. If you search "Bach" on YouTube you get a new video every 3 minutes. Each 6 minutes and 12 seconds long on average. This means by the time you finish watching one video and move on to the next you'll find two new videos of Bach performances. So the sound of Bach performances won't stop during the child's lifetime and will continue eternally till the end of the world. Wait, did you just say "eternally till the end of the world"? You mean if the world ends eternity will end too? No, I mean that the eternity of this world will end. When one world ends another world begins its own eternity. That world has its own Bach, and that composer writing the same pieces as Bach might go by the name of Kim Geumsongyi. Bach dies, a Mozart by the name of Yoo Ji-hye is born, people like you and I coming up with these cursed experiments are born, people invent videos and YouTube, and a child might be born to listen to all the music and watch all the videos that come up when you search "Kim Geumsongyi." That child would perceive Kim Geumsongyi's music as all the sounds of the world. The child would pronounce the word "eternity" as an interval in a Kim Geumsongyi piece. Music, for this child, would be the chewing sound coming from its mouth during the two meals provided every day. Music, for this child, would be the void created by the F sharp absent from the piece. But this experiment has ethical issues. I know that. And this other world has its own guy wearing glasses botching the cantata and struggling to fix the F sharp on the Yamaha, and that's me. I called it quits and left. Bach's full name was Johann Sebastian Bach. Right? Or was it Johann Strines Bach? Wait, is Bach pronounced "Bahhh"? Bach, Bach. Wow, it's so cool by the river, even in the summer. Where should we go next? The arcade? The beach, at night? Your place?

Formless gift exchange party

Biki feels that his place is cramped
for Biki has a history
and this history fills Biki's place
Living in Biki's history
are Biki's friends
whose friend faces
whose friend gestures
whose friend laughter
are ghosts haunting Biki's place
When Biki moves they tag along

Biki lives in Yeonnam-dong
Biki has moved several times in Yeonnam-dong

next to Palette*
across Palette
west of Palette
east of Palette
to the North Pole of Yeonnam-dong
to the South Pole of Yeonnam-dong
None of Biki's friends know how many times
Biki's moved
But many of Biki's friends
know what Biki likes
And so Biki's house
is crowded with stuff, such as

* Palette is the name of a bar in Yeonnam-dong. Biki worked there as a bartender for 4 years.

a collected Haruki

a Lush bath bomb

a Tom Waits vinyl

a Kuang Program cassette

a group photo from The House of Mirth

Kim Sono's first poetry collection

Kim Sono's second poetry collection

a sofa slightly too hard to sleep on

a plastic bathtub found on the first floor

a moka pot

a picture frame from France

a pea pod plush?

(Oh, the one Biki got for me on Halloween eight years ago on a Hongdae street)

Biki says
For this housewarming party
I will only accept formless gifts
I am exhausted by all this stuff

Huh?
Formless gifts?

His friends begin thinking
We've got to get Biki
formless things
but what could those things be . . .

Such things as

a prayer for Biki's past and future
a large loaf of bread we can all share
jokes
life updates
indemnity insurance
showing up in a cool outfit
breakdancing
an e-ticket for a flight
next month's rent
room cleaning service
a soft voice
a piano performance
a good luck spell

Instead of all these things I
decide to gift Biki a poem
and this is that poem

The poem is filling up this piece of paper,
so I wonder if it counts as a formless thing?
I hesitate a bit
but decide to bring it anyway
One piece of paper
Let's just call it formless
If the piece of paper is too big or too heavy
the poem can be copied into a computer
If it runs out of memory
the poem can be memorized

Then Biki can recite the poem wherever
without this piece of paper
And so this piece of paper
is a brief form en route to formlessness,
a temporary form

Biki doesn't work at Palette anymore
He works at Midnight Pleasure
Biki's government name is Jo Daehyeon
When calling out to Biki
we might say
Daehyeon!
we might also say
Biki!

Either way Biki turns around
with the face we remember
the face with form
just like that

When I'm writing like this

You peel an apple for me
When I'm writing like this
You turn my desk
An inch closer to the window
When I'm writing like this
You tear a piece of sky and
Leave it in my pencil case
When I'm writing like this
You don't speak at all
Sometimes you don't even leave
When I'm writing like this
You hum
And you watch
The garden birds

Their feet dallying all day
But the birds leave
When I'm writing like this
You turn down the TV
Leaving the typhoon forecast
Locked in that silence
When I'm writing like this
You lie on a gray sofa
When I'm writing like this
The sound of candle wax
Falls deep
Into your sleep
When I'm writing like this
You must be suffering a burn

When I'm writing like this
Writing of a distant typhoon
Writing that it's coming
When I'm writing like this
When I'm like this

POET'S NOTE

Poems Holding Almost Nothing

I am sitting at a desk. I have a book, a piece of paper, and a pen. I open the book. I read it. I copy it by hand. But the pen holds no ink. Nothing gets written on the piece of paper. And yet, I read. And I copy. Still nothing written on the paper. The tip of the pen leaves etches. Sometimes it leaves nothing at all.

The poems in *Syncopation* paint alongside the trajectory of the book, forming a sequence. My writing process was as follows: First I'd write a poem. I'd write something that might be considered a poem. Then I'd use the ending of that poem to begin the next poem. The ending of that next poem would begin the one after that.

This simple constraint brought many questions. Where does the ending itself begin and end? That was one of the easier questions. What is an ending? It could be a word or a sentence or a movement before it turns into a sentence or a layer of the thick imagery brought forth by a word; it could be a rhythm or part of a rhythm or an attitude or a will or a face. If the so-called "ending" of one poem could operate as the beginning of the next, must this connection be exposed or explicated at all? A poem could be exaggerated or seen in a different light or dragged into some strange place by the poem after it. A poem could keep dancing with the poem before it or tie up its body. And so on . . .

The constraint generated more and more possibilities for my writing. I must confess that this excess of possibilities truly annoyed me. Too many possibilities exist in this world, and perhaps we briefly hold the world in place with our existence and our movement. Perhaps poetry, like the world, is an emptiness too large and wide, tied into shape only when it is read. Thoughts like these may or may not have crossed my mind.

If one poem can be used to create the next, what is held in a poem?

(A bit irresponsible of me to say this after posing so many questions, but) I hate questions. I want the world to be all answers. I hate the intentions behind questions and the demands made by questions and the fingers pointed by questions. What's worse, questions are difficult to forget.

Writing these poems, I had to forget my questions. To forget, I imagined a humming sound. Rhythmic humming, wrinkled humming, shattered humming. Humming in an empty house where no one is listening. Sound carried over into simultaneous activities like cleaning or walking. Sound without destination. Sound resisting domination or reduction. Leaking from a dark mouth as the outside world rumbles and tumbles on. Containing just enough willpower for a lullaby that puts a loved one to sleep. Lacking any composition, form, or meaning. Barely hitting the right notes. Holding almost nothing. Without lyrics, without a score. But musical, for a brief moment on a sunny day.

If only such humming could continue along a hypothetical line. I had to give that line a close look.

Sometimes I'd revise my existing poems to fit the sequence, fixing their beginnings and endings. It was as if strange holes were appearing on the fronts and backs of those poems.

Whenever I struggled to dial my assumptions about poetry back to zero, whenever I applied force in the opposite direction of fixedness, my force would be scattered by yet another force. This counterforce preceded both the mind and the body. While my formal constraint, a word chain of sorts, exerted pressure throughout the collection, I think I wanted that pressure to rupture and puncture space rather than seal or condense it, and I wanted this hole to open towards a road. On it, I wanted letters to flow. I think I wanted chance and spontaneity to loosen and widen the closing gaps between words—but here, again, I was left feeling unsure.

And so I returned to the idea of humming. Faintly and foolishly persisting. Almost nothing yet definitely something.

*

The word "humming" might be an entrance to this collection. Why can't the entirety of a space be an entrance? I might ask here. Humming, humming, I repeat to myself and feel little bees buzzing around my lips.

Some images trickled into the poems, creating thin ripples, the way a song you heard in the past might turn into a tune you hum. I wrote "The red behind my eyelids" after wondering for a long time why my first memory is of my grandmother's face with a bloody nose, and whether this had actually happened. I decided to bring these questions to a poem.

Writing "Like beauty without content," I received the help of many. In a workshop on doodling, my friend Moon Boyoung suggested that we translate a poem by the poet Kim Jong-sam. ("Walkology" is my imitation of Boyoung from the same workshop.) The form of "Like beauty without content" takes inspiration from Ocean

Vuong's "Seventh Circle of Earth" in *Night Sky With Exit Wounds*. The fifth footnote quotes and paraphrases parts of critic Ryu Hangil's lecture "Time: Documentation and Speed - Rhythm Machine :: Documentation Experienced :: Feedback," held in February 2024 at SPACE ÆFTER. Whether it's an accurate paraphrase I don't know. Many thanks to poet Kim Jong-sam.

The night after I wrote "A soft greeting," Seonju unni appeared in my dream. We put our arms around each other's shoulders and walked down a road. Unni made a joke that was familiar to us both. Only after I woke up did I realize this joke was a sentence from "A soft greeting." That had to be unni's joke. Unni came to my dream to read this poem to me in her own voice.

"Formless gift exchange party" celebrates the birthday and move of my old friend Kim Biki in 2024. To Biki, and to friends in the black-and-white photograph at the House of Mirth;

To my good friend and translator Eunice, who, at our New York poetry reading, sat beside me and read aloud "The red behind my eyelids" and "The boundary as an aesthetic choice"; to Newlines; to white-haired Leslie Cheung; to the faded names of childhood friends who played the ABC game with me; to Doyi, the very first reader of all the poems in this collection; to my teacher, So Yeon, who called me Sono for the first time in a dark stairwell; to Grandma, who held me in her arms even as her nose bled; to my family, about whom I wrote poems for the first time; to friends, near and far, who wave at me; to clouds of faces; and

to Liyoun;

To those who have stayed, even in these poems holding almost nothing,

I send my love and thanks.

POET'S ESSAY

A Medley of Lullabies and a Single-Song Universe

I flew a lot this year and last year. I was always sitting in a chair, and if I could erase the plane from the scene, I would have looked like a slouched figure, knees bent, floating midair. The clouds outside my window were floating just like me. The clouds were scattering, and I was scattering myself, too, at a slower pace. I was carried at high speed. And I managed to sleep. It is strange that one can sleep in the sky. While I slept, light spread on my skin and sneaked through my eyelids, limning the objects in my dream. The clouds seeped into the whites of my eyes. If you experience reality too deeply, it turns into fantasy. Language hauls me into the depths of the fantasy that is reality. Time doesn't flow, according to the laws of physics, but we say that "time flows."

*

Wat Mahathat, a temple near Bangkok, holds rows of headless Buddha statues. They were beheaded long ago by Burmese troops invading the Kingdom of Siam. The headless Buddhas stand along the rectangular borders of the great temple. Take one step forward, and you find a headless Buddha. Two steps forward, and you find another. I conjured up the faces of people I knew in place of the missing heads. Buddhism teaches that if you meet a Buddha you must kill the Buddha. But I had to lower my head in reverence towards these headless statues. I laid my hand on a statue's open palm. Made of black stone, the palm was warm under the Thai sun.

Behind one of the temple gates stood a banyan tree. Entangled in its roots was a Buddha head. A single head to restore the heads on all the other statues.

*

Last night, lying down to sleep, I felt a splitting pain in my hands and feet. The past is lying somewhere, embodied in a specific form. The future is also lying somewhere, but the body simply hasn't traveled through that place. When my subconscious becomes temporarily accessible I can experience the moment I travel through death but if that moment I've always feared is the transition from existence to nonexistence then perhaps I'll continue to exist somewhere in the universe in the form of small scattered particles carrying this life, I think, then go on YouTube to watch an interview with director Apichatpong Weerasethakul. His films slide free from the atrocities of time, transform the residues of dreams into aspects of reality, assign greater credibility to scatters of ghosts than to gods, and drive narratives towards a tangible presence. His pure optimism consoles me.

I've decided I should quit meditating for a while.

*

In the ancient Kingdom of Lanna in northern

Thailand, there were three genders: male, female, and a third gender. Women stayed at home to raise the children and men went out to seek food. And those of the third gender taught the children.

Someone in a pink polo shirt said this to us and disappeared.

*

One day and night of the god Brahma lasts 8.64 billion human years, which is longer than the Earth or Sun has existed, and amounts to half of the time since the Big Bang. Hinduism is a religion preoccupied with the notion that the universe experiences infinite cycles of deaths and rebirths. The universe is but a god's dream;

after one hundred Brahmic years, Brahma enters a dreamless sleep, dissolving both the universe and himself. After another Brahmic century, the god rises from his sleep, rebuilds himself, and resumes his dream of the lotus universe.

In Hinduism, the creator and the destroyer are the same god. Human beings are the dreams of gods; gods, too, are the dreams of human beings. The cycles of creation and destruction are rhythmic; the universe is a single song.

*

My pet kitten keeps waking up. A lullaby can put it back to sleep. After I sing a medley of all the lullabies I know, I find myself before a white boat quivering like a balloon full of water. In the sleeping face of the kitten, I see the sleeping faces of countless babies. I listen to countless lullabies that were sung to put countless faces to sleep. In rooms. In parks. In trains. On battlefields. On that baby blue blanket from my childhood. All lullabies are sung in similar voices. If there were to be a hypothetical notebook recording the waveform of every lullaby ever sung, the waves of several melodies would overlap. These would be the patterns of sleep. Vibrations imitating sleep to bring sleep. Sleep can be understood through lullabies.

*

Textbytexture's bio is as follows:

To write a poem is to arrange words on paper

in a strange and subtle way, producing a single original and exclusive record. Such records, as they are created and received, generate various interpretations and images. But the words become fixed and solidified when they are engraved on paper. Paradoxically, this limits the potentiality of language to be spoken, transformed, and expanded. The act of writing a poem entails a loss of, and nostalgia for, language—we believe that this property of language has to do with its physicality, or its dependence on human bodies and lives. When language manifests itself as layers of images free from signification, rather than as words written on paper, language behaves as variable and fluid matter, ready to form new relationships with the world.

When we look at an image, language operates through individual interpretation, existing within each viewer. When we read a text, on the other hand, images operate through individual interpretation, existing within each reader. We hope to explore these relations between image and text, which are antithetical yet inseparable; hypothesize fissures between the two; and explore the ruptures and chain reactions that take place when these oppositions are subverted. We also focus on the social and political implications of our methodology, because the double movements of text and image ask that we see the world as a place with unfixed, pliable, and dynamic boundaries.

COMMENTARY

K
POET

At Last, the Sound of Laughter

Song Seung eon (Poet)

The profane world was, if not silent, quiet. And if we think of "noise" in its less pejorative sense as any big sound, the coupling of noise and sacred is easier to interpret.

—R. Murray Schafer, *The Soundscape: Our Sonic Environment and the Tuning of the World* (Korean translation: Geumulko Books, 2008)

R. Murray Schafer has explored in depth how sound affects human behavior, and how landscapes emerge through sound. He refers to sounds that form relationships with humankind as "a whole new world," and to humankind as the creators of this world. Reading this, I thought, *Here's a crazy conductor trying to make the universe his orchestra.*

Kim Sono's third poetry collection awakened my memory of Schafer, by an association that was not entirely illogical or subconscious. Countless sounds can be heard in the tunnel traveling through these poems, and among these various sounds is one that continues to overlap and reverberate: the sound of laughter.

Why do I hear laughter in this collection? This isn't to say that Kim Sono's previous two collections don't laugh at all. It's that those two more often feel like silent smiles. Like "your" smile shining too bright in the light reflected off a silver gum wrapper ("Gum Wrapper"). Smiles like this feel more like carefully staged scenes. *Syncopation* is similar to these earlier collections, but also differs from them quite a deal, in that it captures less embellished everyday noises like the ones you might hear in a raw video essay—as I go on I shall consider why I feel this way.

When reading Kim Sono's poems, I first pay attention to the objects that participate in them. This is to contextualize them in past relationships Kim Sono has formed with their poetic objects. Sometimes the poems involve the traditional "I" speaker observing the object; at other times, they express discomfort with this dynamic (or boredom with first-person speech), and when this happens the poet tends to give up the first person and let subject and object switch places. In their first collection *Night Soccer* (Achimdal Books, 2020), where the "I" speaker has a relatively more established presence, there is one poem where this reversed approach is evident. The poem "Rain and Meat" features meat, or nonhuman animals made edible, in lieu of an "I" or "you." On a rainy day, pieces of meat walk in the streets, letting their blood flow into the drain, umbrellas in hand. The inverted dynamic of this poem, as well as the transformation of its objects, ruthlessly exposes the violent consumption and exploitation of nonhuman beings.

The next collection, *The Film Set* (Moonji Books, 2022), goes beyond these substitutions and further interrogates the idea of the "I" speaker itself, and lets speakers behave with greater flexibility. Instead of a dominating "I" speaker, there are various objects escaping their objecthood and invading the territory of the subject. "Wooden Hotel" is one such poem. The moment "I" sit down, the room begins to turn itself into a mess. The sea swims away from the sea and the shirt trips over the shirt. The lobby isn't located next to the room, but *sitting* next to the room. Things and situations that are meant to be objects try to seize "my" position as the speaker, leaving "me" with a kind of motion sickness.

With some subtle differences, the two collections treat their objects in more or less similar ways. Speakers and objects maintain a certain distance, always on edge. Here I turn to the ways in which *Syncopation* feels different. In this collection, the "I" speaker and objects often follow and mingle with each other, instead of competing or tensing up.

Because the cloth, the wall, and the outside world are all in the color white, a sense of ambiguity surrounds them ("Like cloud like wall"); "our" laughter is indistinguishable from the stir of the trees ("A weak unsettled life"); gusts of snow and "I" fall on each other ("Coming before going"); it's unclear if that slanting shadow is the cloud's or the gate's, and "I become Unni and then me. Then a friend who might be Unni" ("A soft greeting"). Objects, which used to be sorted and named according to their purposes, are now difficult to tell apart. Perhaps this is because many of these poems take place in the liminal space between dreams and reality. Dreams, of course, are difficult to control. Having lost control over their surroundings, the speaker of "Things hard to tell apart in the dark" simply accepts countless objects as they rain down, like rays of light or drops of water, and plays games with them. That game—bringing your palms together, twisting your palms against each other, then opening and showing both palms—seems to be a strange and mysterious ritual erasing the hierarchy or distinction between the "I" speaker and the objects.

There is less tension created by distance; the form also changes into a less formal outfit, ready to have fun. In a lighter and more relaxed atmosphere, one poem takes the form of a brief utterance to an unspecified addressee ("No"); another borrows lines from Kim Jong-sam's "Drummer Boy," scatters numbers across the blank page like a blizzard, then fills the footnotes with all the content ("Like beauty without content").

The speaker observes the object from a shorter distance; the two move in and out of each other, flexibly and harmoniously. In a world that was once cold and dry, lightness and warmth arrive like new seasons. This scene is different from those of Kim Sono's earlier poems. Perhaps it has to do with "the realization that life and poetry are not very different from each other," as the poet said elsewhere. But Kim Sono might not necessarily continue to take this approach. As the title of the collection suggests, the poet is aware of the exceptionality of this moment. Syncopation is a kind of variation that breaks the basic rules of rhythm. A deviation that brings surprise and energy. And so this collection, seen from afar, might be a "syncopation" among other collections that have been or will be written by Kim Sono.

But it's more than just the warmth of this world that creates the sound of laughter. It's necessary to find out where the laughter is coming from. To do so, ironically, one must examine images of death. This collection has several, and so do the poet's other collections. But because the poet's relationship with objects has changed since, so must their death imagery. "The red behind my eyelids" captures the speaker's childhood memory. The young speaker is at home waiting for their grandmother, playing with a warm square of light. The grandmother soon arrives. Her nose is bleeding. This is the first time the speaker sees blood in their life.

In what could be a scary and horrible moment, the grandmother smiles, for some reason, as she wipes her blood. The blood (evoking that of Christ) dyes the square of light, adding a troubling air of sacredness to the memory. There is death behind this smile, but in a way that can easily be misunderstood. The smiles and laughter in this collection are not rendered tragic or heavy by the death behind them. Rather, it is death that lightens and brightens them. Life always shines alongside death like a backlight, and the two are always one in human life—Kim Sono seems to accept this fact with their whole body. In a similar way, we are wounded by the deaths of those around us, and those wounds heal without our knowing ("A certain nuance").

Acceptance. We are all walking in a tunnel that leads to eternity. If we accept this, we can laugh. "Ha ha ha ha" goes the sound ("Same boat different sea"), an ecstatic burst of noise following the realization that all these objects and "I," all the deaths of past and future generations, and everything including "my" own death and the bananas and the soccer balls, are flowing towards a great reunion. In life, a meditation at once long and short, "I" am a place. A boundary at the intersection of objects, dreams and reality, light and darkness, everything. "I" am a channel for sensations, and "I" feel them moving in and moving out. With eardrums and optic nerves and various other sensory organs. When "I" feel the world enter through "my" breath ("It was burdensome trying to become myself"), the soul's gaze transcends the limitations of time and space, traveling across the past, present, and future, through life and death ("A bit of the forest").

Strident laughter. "You" and "I," life and death, harmonize. This laughter, these sacred noises rising upward—how can they not be joyful?

Noise is followed by silence. The poem "Silence" begins in an empty lot and directs its gaze at various sights, which are possibly related to the speaker's everyday activities. The sights behave like noises filling the silent lot—this feels like a natural comparison, given how sound waves can turn into light, or how the poem eventually bursts into sunset colors in the third stanza. Because the empty lot is a spatial silence, it invites countless noises. Because our lives have no public significance, we can assign to it countless private meanings. According to Schafer, this is the layer of sacredness added to our trivial and profane lives. I'm glad to have had this conversation with you, though briefly, about the laughter Kim Sono has let me hear. I hope you and I encounter different stories in this collection, and that you let yours be heard. This will bring more plenitude to Kim Sono's poems.

Where are they headed now? What scenes will

they bring back? I wonder. Kim Sono says they can't show me that road, nor describe it, and all I can do is follow them ("No"). I think I will.

PRAISES FOR KIM SONO

Nonbinary identity cannot be confined to a category. Nonbinary lives resist being forced into a subject's objectifying perception. Centripetal and centrifugal tensions occur around attempts to regulate meaning; people who encounter nonbinary individuals must find themselves in perceptual instability. If it is unknown whether a speaker is human or nonhuman, the identity of their listener also becomes less knowable. [...] At one corner of *The Film Set* lives a community of nonbinary ghosts. As they become poetic quasi-objects, they offer rough sketches of their ghost world. Their ghost voices interrogate natural categories as well as their limitations.

–Jeon Seung-min, in "All of You, Minus Me," a critical introduction to *The Film Set* (Moonji Books, 2022)

K-POET

Syncopation

Written by Kim Sono
Translated by Eunice Lee
Published by ASIA Publishers
Address 445, Hoedong-gil, Paju-si, Gyeonggi-do, Korea
(Seoul Office: 161-1, Seodal-ro, Dongjak-gu,Seoul, Korea)
Email bookasia@hanmail.net
ISBN 979-11-5662-317-5 (set) | 979-11-5662-714-2 (04810)
First published in Korea by ASIA Publishers 2024

*This book is published with the support of the Literature Translation Institute of Korea (LTI Korea).

바이링궐 에디션 한국 대표 소설

한국문학의 가장 중요하고 첨예한 문제의식을 가진 작가들의 대표작을 주제별로 선정!
하버드 한국학 연구원 및 세계 각국의 한국문학 전문 번역진이 참여한 번역 시리즈!
미국 하버드대학교와 컬럼비아대학교 동아시아학과, 캐나다 브리티시컬럼비아대학교 아시아학과 등 해외 대학에서 교재로 채택!

바이링궐 에디션 한국 대표 소설 set 1

분단 Division

01 병신과 머저리-**이청준** The Wounded-**Yi Cheong-jun**
02 어둠의 혼-**김원일** Soul of Darkness-**Kim Won-il**
03 순이삼촌-**현기영** Sun-i Samch'on-**Hyun Ki-young**
04 엄마의 말뚝 1-**박완서** Mother's Stake I-**Park Wan-suh**
05 유형의 땅-**조정래** The Land of the Banished-**Jo Jung-rae**

산업화 Industrialization

06 무진기행-**김승옥** Record of a Journey to Mujin-**Kim Seung-ok**
07 삼포 가는 길-**황석영** The Road to Sampo-**Hwang Sok-yong**
08 아홉 켤레의 구두로 남은 사내-**윤흥길** The Man Who Was Left as Nine Pairs of Shoes-**Yun Heung-gil**
09 돌아온 우리의 친구-**신상웅** Our Friend's Homecoming-**Shin Sang-ung**
10 원미동 시인-**양귀자** The Poet of Wŏnmi-dong-**Yang Kwi-ja**

여성 Women

11 중국인 거리-**오정희** Chinatown-**Oh Jung-hee**
12 풍금이 있던 자리-**신경숙** The Place Where the Harmonium Was-**Shin Kyung-sook**
13 하나코는 없다-**최윤** The Last of Hanak'o-**Ch'oe Yun**
14 인간에 대한 예의-**공지영** Human Decency-**Gong Ji-young**
15 빈처-**은희경** Poor Man's Wife-**Eun Hee-kyung**

바이링궐 에디션 한국 대표 소설 set 2

자유 Liberty

16 필론의 돼지-**이문열** Pilon's Pig-**Yi Mun-yol**
17 슬로우 불릿-**이대환** Slow Bullet-**Lee Dae-hwan**
18 직선과 독가스-**임철우** Straight Lines and Poison Gas-**Lim Chul-woo**
19 깃발-**홍희담** The Flag-**Hong Hee-dam**
20 새벽 출정-**방현석** Off to Battle at Dawn-**Bang Hyeon-seok**

사랑과 연애 Love and Love Affairs

21 별을 사랑하는 마음으로-**윤후명** With the Love for the Stars-**Yun Hu-myong**
22 목련공원-**이승우** Magnolia Park-**Lee Seung-u**
23 칼에 찔린 자국-**김인숙** Stab-**Kim In-suk**
24 회복하는 인간-**한강** Convalescence-**Han Kang**
25 트렁크-**정이현** In the Trunk-**Jeong Yi-hyun**

남과 북 South and North

26 판문점-**이호철** Panmunjom-**Yi Ho-chol**
27 수난 이대-**하근찬** The Suffering of Two Generations-**Ha Geun-chan**
28 분지-**남정현** Land of Excrement-**Nam Jung-hyun**
29 봄 실상사-**정도상** Spring at Silsangsa Temple-**Jeong Do-sang**
30 은행나무 사랑-**김하기** Gingko Love-**Kim Ha-kee**

바이링궐 에디션 한국 대표 소설 set 3

서울 Seoul

31 눈사람 속의 검은 항아리-**김소진** The Dark Jar within the Snowman-**Kim So-jin**
32 오후, 가로지르다-**하성란** Traversing Afternoon-**Ha Seong-nan**
33 나는 봉천동에 산다-**조경란** I Live in Bongcheon-dong-**Jo Kyung-ran**
34 그렇습니까? 기린입니다-**박민규** Is That So? I'm A Giraffe-**Park Min-gyu**
35 성탄특선-**김애란** Christmas Specials-**Kim Ae-ran**

전통 Tradition

36 무자년의 가을 사흘-**서정인** Three Days of Autumn, 1948-**Su Jung-in**
37 유자소전-**이문구** A Brief Biography of Yuja-**Yi Mun-gu**
38 향기로운 우물 이야기-**박범신** The Fragrant Well-**Park Bum-shin**
39 월행-**송기원** A Journey under the Moonlight-**Song Ki-won**
40 협죽도 그늘 아래-**성석제** In the Shade of the Oleander-**Song Sok-ze**

아방가르드 Avant-garde

41 아겔다마-**박상륭** Akeldama-**Park Sang-ryoong**
42 내 영혼의 우물-**최인석** A Well in My Soul-**Choi In-seok**
43 당신에 대해서-**이인성** On You-**Yi In-seong**
44 회색 時-**배수아** Time In Gray-**Bae Su-ah**
45 브라운 부인-**정영문** Mrs. Brown-**Jung Young-moon**

바이링궐 에디션 한국 대표 소설 set 4

디아스포라 Diaspora

46 속옷-**김남일** Underwear-**Kim Nam-il**
47 상하이에 두고 온 사람들-**공선옥** People I Left in Shanghai-**Gong Sun-ok**
48 모두에게 복된 새해-**김연수** Happy New Year to Everyone-**Kim Yeon-su**
49 코끼리-**김재영** The Elephant-**Kim Jae-young**
50 먼지별-**이경** Dust Star-**Lee Kyung**

가족 Family

51 혜자의 눈꽃-**천승세** Hye-ja's Snow-Flowers-**Chun Seung-sei**
52 아베의 가족-**전상국** Ahbe's Family-**Jeon Sang-guk**
53 문 앞에서-**이동하** Outside the Door-**Lee Dong-ha**
54 그리고, 축제-**이혜경** And Then the Festival-**Lee Hye-kyung**
55 봄밤-**권여선** Spring Night-**Kwon Yeo-sun**

유머 Humor

56 오늘의 운세-**한창훈** Today's Fortune-**Han Chang-hoon**
57 새-**전성태** Bird-**Jeon Sung-tae**
58 밀수록 다시 가까워지는-**이기호** So Far, and Yet So Near-**Lee Ki-ho**
59 유리방패-**김중혁** The Glass Shield-**Kim Jung-hyuk**
60 전당포를 찾아서-**김종광** The Pawnshop Chase-**Kim Chong-kwang**

바이링궐 에디션 한국 대표 소설 set 5

관계 Relationship

61 도둑견습 – **김주영** Robbery Training-**Kim Joo-young**
62 사랑하라, 희망 없이 – **윤영수** Love, Hopelessly-**Yun Young-su**
63 봄날 오후, 과부 셋 – **정지아** Spring Afternoon, Three Widows-**Jeong Ji-a**
64 유턴 지점에 보물지도를 묻다 - **윤성희** Burying a Treasure Map at the U-turn-**Yoon Sung-hee**
65 쁘이거나 쯔이거나 - **백가흠** Puy, Thuy, Whatever-**Paik Ga-huim**

일상의 발견 Discovering Everyday Life

66 나는 음식이다 – **오수연** I Am Food-**Oh Soo-yeon**
67 트럭 – **강영숙** Truck-**Kang Young-sook**
68 통조림 공장 - **편혜영** The Canning Factory-**Pyun Hye-young**
69 꽃 – **부희령** Flowers-**Pu Hee-ryoung**
70 피의일요일 – **윤이형** BloodySunday-**Yun I-hyeong**

금기와 욕망 Taboo and Desire

71 북소리 - **송영** Drumbeat-**Song Yong**
72 발칸의 장미를 내게 주었네 - **정미경** He Gave Me Roses of the Balkans-**Jung Mi-kyung**
73 아무도 돌아오지 않는 밤 - **김숨** The Night Nobody Returns Home-**Kim Soom**
74 젓가락여자 - **천운영** Chopstick Woman-**Cheon Un-yeong**
75 아직 일어나지 않은 일 - **김미월** What Has Yet to Happen-**Kim Mi-wol**

바이링궐 에디션 한국 대표 소설 set 6

운명 Fate

76 언니를 놓치다 - **이경자** Losing a Sister-**Lee Kyung-ja**
77 아들 - **윤정모** Father and Son-**Yoon Jung-mo**
78 명두 - **구효서** Relics-**Ku Hyo-seo**
79 모독 - **조세희** Insult-**Cho Se-hui**
80 화요일의 강 - **손홍규** Tuesday River-**Son Hong-gyu**

미의 사제들 Aesthetic Priests

81 고수 - **이외수** Grand Master-**Lee Oisoo**
82 말을 찾아서 - **이순원** Looking for a Horse-**Lee Soon-won**
83 상춘곡 - **윤대녕** Song of Everlasting Spring-**Youn Dae-nyeong**
84 삭매와 자미 - **김별아** Sakmae and Jami-**Kim Byeol-ah**
85 저만치 혼자서 - **김훈** Alone Over There-**Kim Hoon**

식민지의 벌거벗은 자들 The Naked in the Colony

86 감자 - **김동인** Potatoes-**Kim Tong-in**
87 운수 좋은 날 - **현진건** A Lucky Day-**Hyŏn Chin'gŏn**
88 탈출기 - **최서해** Escape-**Ch'oe So-hae**
89 과도기 - **한설야** Transition-**Han Seol-ya**
90 지하촌 - **강경애** The Underground Village-**Kang Kyŏng-ae**

바이링궐 에디션 한국 대표 소설 set 7

백치가 된 식민지 지식인 Colonial Intellectuals Turned "Idiots"

91 날개 - **이상** Wings-**Yi Sang**
92 김 강사와 T 교수 - **유진오** Lecturer Kim and Professor T-**Chin-O Yu**
93 소설가 구보씨의 일일 - **박태원** A Day in the Life of Kubo the Novelist-**Pak Taewon**
94 비 오는 길 - **최명익** Walking in the Rain-**Ch'oe Myŏngik**
95 빛 속에 - **김사량** Into the Light-**Kim Sa-ryang**

한국의 잃어버린 얼굴 Traditional Korea's Lost Faces

96 봄·봄 – **김유정** Spring, Spring–**Kim Yu-jeong**
97 벙어리 삼룡이 – **나도향** Samnyong the Mute–**Na Tohyang**
98 달밤 – **이태준** An Idiot's Delight–**Yi T'ae-jun**
99 사랑손님과 어머니 – **주요섭** Mama and the Boarder–**Chu Yo-sup**
100 갯마을 – **오영수** Seaside Village–**Oh Yeongsu**

해방 전후(前後) Before and After Liberation

101 소망 – **채만식** Juvesenility–**Ch'ae Man-Sik**
102 두 파산 – **염상섭** Two Bankruptcies–**Yom Sang-Seop**
103 풀잎 – **이효석** Leaves of Grass–**Lee Hyo-seok**
104 맥 – **김남천** Barley–**Kim Namch'on**
105 꺼삐딴 리 – **전광용** Kapitan Ri–**Chŏn Kwangyong**

전후(戰後) Korea After the Korean War

106 소나기 – **황순원** The Cloudburst–**Hwang Sun-Won**
107 등신불 – **김동리** Tŭngsin-bul–**Kim Tong-ni**
108 요한 시집 – **장용학** The Poetry of John–**Chang Yong-hak**
109 비 오는 날 – **손창섭** Rainy Days–**Son Chang-sop**
110 오발탄 – **이범선** A Stray Bullet–**Lee Beomseon**